A Guide to
AMERICAN STATES

Ohio

THE BUCKEYE STATE

MEDIA ENHANCED BOOKS
AV2
BY WEIGL
ADDED VALUE • AUDIO VISUAL

www.av2books.com

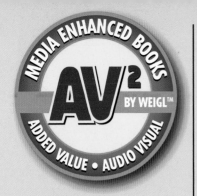

AV² provides enriched content that supplements and complements this book. Weigl's AV² books strive to create inspired learning and engage young minds in a total learning experience.

Your AV² Media Enhanced books come alive with...

Audio
Listen to sections of the book read aloud.

Key Words
Study vocabulary, and complete a matching word activity.

Go to **www.av2books.com**, and enter this book's unique code.

Video
Watch informative video clips.

Quizzes
Test your knowledge.

BOOK CODE

Q662272

Embedded Weblinks
Gain additional information for research.

Slide Show
View images and captions, and prepare a presentation.

AV² by Weigl brings you media enhanced books that support active learning.

Try This!
Complete activities and hands-on experiments.

... and much, much more!

Published by AV² by Weigl
350 5ᵗʰ Avenue, 59ᵗʰ Floor
New York, NY 10118
Website: www.av2books.com   www.weigl.com

Library of Congress Cataloging-in-Publication Data

Lawton, Val.
 Ohio / Val Lawton.
    p. cm. -- (A guide to American states)
Includes index.
 ISBN 978-1-61690-807-2 (hardcover : alk. paper) -- ISBN 978-1-61690-483-8 (online)
1. Ohio--Juvenile literature. I. Title.
 F491.3.L393 2011
 977.1--dc23
                          2011019029

Printed in the United States of America in North Mankato, Minnesota

052011
WEP180511

Project Coordinator Jordan McGill
Art Director Terry Paulhus

Photo Credits
Every reasonable effort has been made to trace ownership and to obtain permission to reprint copyright material. The publishers would be pleased to have any errors or omissions brought to their attention so that they may be corrected in subsequent printings.

Weigl acknowledges Getty Images as its primary image supplier for this title.

Contents

AV² Book Code..................................... 2

Introduction 4

Where Is Ohio? 6

Mapping Ohio..................................... 8

The Land.. 10

Climate.. 12

Natural Resources.............................. 14

Plants.. 16

Animals.. 18

Tourism.. 20

Industry 22

Goods and Services 24

American Indians............................... 26

Explorers and Missionaries 28

Early Settlers..................................... 30

Notable People 32

Population 34

Politics and Government.................... 36

Cultural Groups................................. 38

Arts and Entertainment.................... 40

Sports 42

National Averages Comparison.......... 44

How to Improve My Community........... 45

Exercise Your Mind!.......................... 46

Words to Know / Index...................... 47

Log on to www.av2books.com................ 48

The Rock and Roll Hall of Fame and Museum, in downtown Cleveland, is visited by more than 8 million people each year.

Introduction

Ohio is a remarkable state, with rich farmland, beautiful scenery, exciting cities, and a well-preserved history. Ohio's geographic location makes the state an important crossroads between the Eastern Seaboard and the Midwest.

Ohio is known for its fertile plains and rolling hills, but the state is also famous for a tall, modern glass building in Cleveland. The Rock and Roll Hall of Fame and Museum showcases rock and roll's great artists, such as Elvis Presley, the Beatles, Elton John, and Aretha Franklin. Many people visit the Rock and Roll Hall of Fame to learn about the musicians who have made rock and roll one of the world's most popular forms of music. Ohio even has an official rock song, "Hang on Sloopy." It was a hit in 1965 for a group from Dayton, the McCoys.

Columbus sits on the banks of the Scioto River. It is the largest city in the world that is named after Christopher Columbus.

Farms are a common sight in the southern and western parts of Ohio.

Many inventions and technological firsts came from Ohio. The state witnessed the birth of electric streetlights, when the world's first commercial arc lamps were installed in a Cleveland park by Charles F. Brush in 1879. Before Henry Ford introduced his first automobile, John Lambert chugged down the streets of Ohio City in 1890 in the nation's first gasoline-powered car. The state also saw the nation's first traffic light, in 1914. In addition, one of the greatest inventions of the 20th century originated in Ohio. The Wright brothers, Orville and Wilbur, designed and built the world's first powered airplane in their Dayton workshop. On December 17, 1903, at the hilly North Carolina beach where they took the plane for testing, Orville managed to get the airplane into the sky for a thrilling 12 seconds! Ohio has the Wright brothers to thank for its place in **aviation** history.

 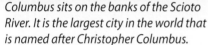

Where Is Ohio?

O hio is part of the central heartland region of the United States called the Midwest. It is the most easterly of the Midwestern states. Ohio borders Michigan and Lake Erie to the north. Kentucky and West Virginia are across the Ohio River to the south and southeast. Indiana is to the west, and Pennsylvania is to the east.

Several riverboats travel the Ohio River today. The first steamboat navigated the river in 1811.

The Roebling Suspension Bridge spans the Ohio River, connecting Cincinnati and Covington, Kentucky. The bridge was built in 1866.

Throughout the state's history, the Ohio River and Lake Erie have been important transportation routes. Toledo and Cleveland are major shipping ports on Lake Erie. Cincinnati, in the southwestern part of the state, grew up around its busy river port on the Ohio River. At several points along the Ohio River, ferries transport cargo and passengers between Ohio and neighboring states.

There are many other ways to reach Ohio. Air travelers can land in many Ohio cities, including Akron, Dayton, and Toledo. The busiest airports in the state are in Cleveland and Columbus. Cincinnati/Northern Kentucky International Airport is located just south of Cincinnati in Hebron, Kentucky. Some of the country's oldest railroad lines cross Ohio, and Amtrak has several passenger routes through the state. For those who prefer to travel by bus or automobile, state and federal highways cross the state in all directions.

I DIDN'T KNOW THAT!

Ohio's official nickname is the Buckeye State in honor of the buckeye tree, which grows throughout the area.

The state motto, "With God, All Things Are Possible," was not adopted until 1959. A 12-year-old boy won a contest sponsored by the state legislature to suggest the motto.

People who live in Ohio are called "Ohioans" or "Buckeyes."

The name Ohio comes from an Iroquois word that means "beautiful river" or "large river."

"Beautiful Ohio," the state song, was originally written about the Ohio River, not the whole state. Lawmakers later adopted a new chorus with lines about Ohio's farms, cities, and industries.

Mapping Ohio

Water is an important part of Ohio's geography, making up much of the state's borders. The Lake Erie shoreline runs for 312 miles to the north, and there are eight ports along the lake in Ohio. Meanwhile, the Ohio River, which is one of the largest rivers in North America, flows for more than 450 miles along the state's southern and southeastern borders. Ohio has more than 3,300 named rivers and streams and more than 60,000 lakes, **reservoirs**, and ponds.

Sites and Symbols

STATE SEAL
Ohio

STATE BIRD
Cardinal

STATE FLOWER
Scarlet carnation

STATE FLAG
Ohio

STATE ANIMAL
White-tailed deer

STATE TREE
Ohio buckeye

Nickname The Buckeye State

Motto With God, All Things Are Possible

Song "Beautiful Ohio," by Ballard MacDonald and Mary Earl

Entered the Union March 1, 1803, as the 17th state

Capital Columbus

Population (2010 Census) 11,536,504 Ranked 7th state

STATE CAPITAL

Columbus became the state capital of Ohio in 1816. Before that time, the towns of Chillicothe and Zanesville had both served as the capital. Columbus was chosen as the site for the new capital because of its central location within the state and access to major river routes.

LEGEND

- —— Road
- —— River
- ⭐ State Capital
- ● City
- ▨ Ohio
- —— State Border

Map Scale

0   50 Miles

N

United States

Hawai'i   Alaska

Ohio

The Land

Ohio is made up of three major land regions. They are the Appalachian Plateau, the Lake Plains, and the Central Plains, also called the Till Plains. The Appalachian Plateau is an area of winding rivers, hills, and hardwood trees that reaches west from Ohio's eastern border. West of the Appalachian Plateau stretch the two lowland areas. The slightly rolling Lake Plains, in the northwestern part of the state, extend along Lake Erie to the Michigan border. The Central Plains, in central-western and southwestern Ohio, provide deep, fertile soil. This region is part of the nation's Corn Belt.

Slow-moving **glaciers** that covered much of North America thousands of years ago are responsible for Ohio's rich soil. Glaciers blanketed about two-thirds of the area that is now Ohio, shaping the land into gently rolling hills as they moved across it. The melting glaciers left swamps and bogs, especially in the northwestern part of the state. Later, when the areas were drained by natural processes or by settlers, fertile soil remained.

KELLEYS ISLAND

Located in Lake Erie, Kelleys Island is known for its unique natural features. They include a limestone cobble beach and abundant red cedar trees.

HOCKING HILLS STATE PARK

This park, in the south-central part of the state, is popular with hikers. The park features spectacular rock formations, deep gorges, cliffs, and waterfalls.

CUYAHOGA VALLEY NATIONAL PARK

The only national park in Ohio, Cuyahoga Valley in the northeast has waterfalls, forests, hills, and ravines. The park surrounds the Cuyahoga River.

CENTRAL PLAINS

Western Ohio has rich, fertile soil. Many farms are located in this region, growing corn, soybeans, and other crops.

I DIDN'T KNOW THAT!

Campbell Hill, in Logan County, is the highest point in Ohio. It is 1,549 feet above sea level.

The Bass Islands are a group of islands located off Ohio's northern coast. They are mostly made of limestone.

Rocky Fork State Park, in southern Ohio, has a 2,080-acre lake. It provides a home for waterfowl and other animals.

At the Glacial Grooves State Memorial, one can see the most dramatic results left by glaciers thousands of years ago. The memorial is located on the north side of Kelleys Island in Lake Erie.

The Lake Plains were once the bottom of a large, ancient lake known as Lake Maumee.

Wayne National Forest in the southeastern part of the state is the only national forest in Ohio.

Flooding is common in parts of Ohio, when heavy rains cause rivers to overflow. More than $240 million in damage occurred during 2007 floods in the state.

Climate

O hio has cold winters and hot, humid summers. There is a large amount of snow in the winter. For many years, Ohio has struggled with spring flooding. Since the early 1900s, Ohioans have widened riverbanks and constructed dams and reservoirs to help manage spring floods.

Average winter temperatures in Ohio range from lows of 16° Fahrenheit to highs of 37° F. The coldest recorded temperature in Ohio was –39° F on February 10, 1899, in the town of Milligan. The warmest recorded temperature was 113° F on July 21, 1934, near Gallipolis. In general, northern Ohio has a mild autumn.

Average Annual Precipitation Across Ohio

The average annual precipitation varies for different cities across Ohio. Which city in the graph below gets the most precipitation? What problems might people have if their city got too much rain, and what could they do to solve these problems?

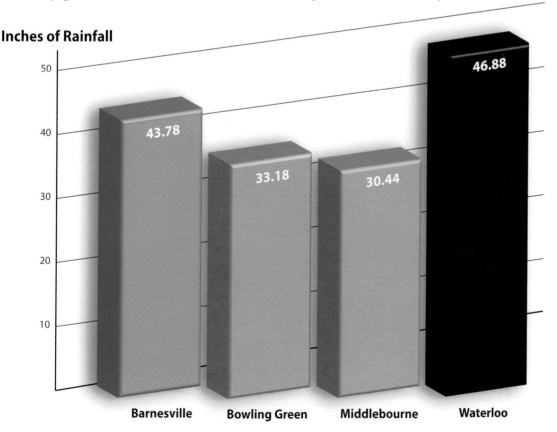

Inches of Rainfall

City	Inches
Barnesville	43.78
Bowling Green	33.18
Middlebourne	30.44
Waterloo	46.88

Natural Resources

O hioans recognized the importance of their mineral resources during the 1800s. Residents discovered that the eastern part of the state sat on large deposits of coal, petroleum, and natural gas. Coal was first found in 1808, and mining soon became a major industry in the state. Coal, petroleum, and natural gas are still found in Ohio. Today, Ohio does not have as much of these resources as it once did, but the state still has an estimated 11.5 billion tons of economically recoverable coal reserves, as well as oil and gas.

Ohio produces more than 42 million tons of limestone each year. It has a value of approximately $390 million.

Many other minerals are taken from the earth for industrial use. Ohio's most important mineral is limestone, and the Buckeye State ranks among the top limestone-producing states in the nation. Limestone is a **sedimentary** rock useful in building materials and industrial processes. Some types of limestone are used in flooring and monuments. Other industrial minerals from Ohio include sand and gravel, salt, sandstone, clay, shale, gypsum, and peat.

Water is another important resource in Ohio. The state's long Lake Erie shoreline contains some of the area's largest cities and heaviest industry. For many years, the water quality in the lake suffered because of industrial pollution. Fish and bird populations had been steadily declining in these waters until efforts were made to clean the lake. By the early 1990s, recreational fishing had resumed along Ohio's shoreline. However, much work remained to fix the damage of previous decades. The Office of Coastal Management was created in the state in 2002 to manage Ohio's Lake Erie resources, monitor activities that affect these resources, and make sure they are used in a way that preserves them.

Coal is mined in the eastern part of the state. Ohio ranks third among all states in the consumption of coal.

Ohio is among the top states in the production of construction sand and gravel.

Most of Ohio's limestone comes from the northwestern and central parts of the state.

The state stone is Ohio flint, a type of quartz that naturally occurs in many colors. American Indians made spear points and arrowheads out of this stone.

Coal is the source of most of the electricity used in Ohio.

Pollution in Lake Erie inspired Dr. Seuss to write the 1971 children's book *The Lorax*, which is about environmental issues.

The Ohio River handles about 275 millions tons of cargo every year, which is more than is handled by the Panama Canal.

Plants

From dense forests to open prairies, Ohio's natural vegetation provides habitats for a large variety of animal life. Forests in Ohio are found primarily in the state's southern and eastern areas. In most of the state, farmland has replaced the original forests. Hardwood trees common to the state include oak, ash, maple, hickory, walnut, and basswood. Virginia pine, white pine, and eastern hemlock are some of the **conifers** that grow in the area. The Ohio buckeye tree, which is the state tree, is found mostly near rivers and in moist areas. It can grow to as tall as 80 feet, and it bears yellow flowers in the spring.

Springtime brings an array of forest wildflowers to Ohio. It is not unusual to spot violets, mayapples, hepaticas, and bloodroot in the spring. In the fall, many wildflowers, such as black-eyed Susans and goldenrods, grow in open spaces.

NORTHERN BLAZING STAR

The northern blazing star grows best in dry, sunny places. This wildflower is not bothered by heat and drought.

BUTTERFLY WEED

The butterfly weed, a common wildflower in Ohio, is also called the orange milkweed. It attracts the caterpillars of Monarch butterflies, which feed on the leaves.

RED MAPLE TREE

Red maple trees are found throughout Ohio, in moist areas of open woodlands and along creeks. The tree can grow up to 70 feet tall and 40 feet wide.

OHIO BUCKEYE TREE

The Ohio buckeye is Ohio's state tree. Its leaves, stems, and flowers can have an unpleasant odor when crushed.

I DIDN'T KNOW THAT!

Before European settlement, 95 percent of Ohio was covered with forests. Today, forests cover only about one-fourth of the land.

Ohio has an official wildflower, the white trillium, which is found in every county in the state.

The azalea is a common shrub in Ohio. Others include the dogwood, hawthorn, viburnum, and sumac.

To preserve trees in Ohio, forest areas have been set aside that are protected by the government. Ohio has 21 state forests.

The Shawnee State Forest was once part of the hunting grounds of the Shawnee Indians. The forest covers 63,000 acres.

The running buffalo clover is the only **endangered** plant **species** in Ohio.

Animals

Ohio was once home to such large mammals as elk, cougars, black bears, timber wolves, and bison, or buffalo. Today, the white-tailed deer is the only native large mammal that is still plentiful in the state. Though they were once hunted nearly to extinction, by the late 20th century, white-tailed deer were found in every Ohio county. Common small animals in the state include cottontail rabbits, beavers, muskrats, raccoons, moles, and opossums.

Because Ohio lies along an important bird migration route, as many as 400 different kinds of birds soar overhead or spend parts of the year in the state. About 180 different bird species are native to Ohio, including wild turkeys, quail, and pheasants. There are also many varieties of fish in the state's lakes and rivers. They include bass, northern pike, walleye, and muskellunge. In the north, Lake Erie is home to walleye, steelhead trout, and yellow perch.

WHITE-TAILED DEER

The official state animal, the white-tailed deer eats a variety of fruits, nuts, grasses, and leaves. The fur of young deer is covered with white spots, which disappear over time.

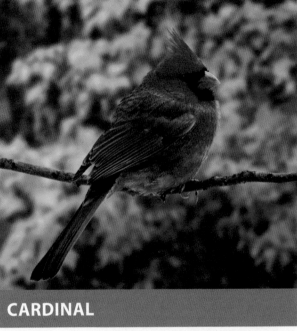

CARDINAL

The state bird of Ohio, the cardinal can be found in all of the state's counties. The male, which is a brilliant red, grows to 8.75 inches long. Cardinals eat insects, seeds, and fruit.

COTTONTAIL RABBIT

The cottontail rabbit is found throughout Ohio. It eats a wide variety of plants, including clover and dandelions, as well as corn and the bark of young trees.

WALLEYE

The walleye, which eats insects and other fish, is a popular game fish in Ohio. The largest one ever caught in Ohio weighed more than 16 pounds and was 33 inches long.

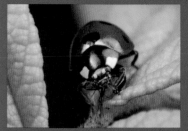

Ohio's state insect is the ladybug.

Eastern timber rattlesnakes, northern copperheads, and eastern massauga rattlesnakes are the only venomous, or poisonous, snakes found in the state.

The black racer snake is the official state reptile.

The Ohio Wildlife Center, which was founded in 1984, cares for all species of injured and orphaned wildlife in the state.

There are a number of endangered animal species in Ohio. They include the Indiana bat, the American burying beetle, and a mussel called the fanshell.

Each year, 1.1 million Ohio sport fishers spend an estimated $1.1 billion on fishing.

Tourism

Ohio is brimming with fascinating sites for visitors to examine. The state has four national historical areas that are within the U.S. National Park system. At Hopewell Culture National Historical Park, visitors can learn about the mound-building American Indians of the Hopewell culture. The other historic sites in Ohio mark and preserve places of national interest. They are the First Ladies National Historic Site, Perry's Victory and International Peace Memorial, and the Dayton Aviation Heritage National Historical Park.

Some tourist attractions in Ohio mark more recent developments. The Rock and Roll Hall of Fame and Museum opened its doors in downtown Cleveland in 1995. Cedar Point, on the shores of Lake Erie in Sandusky, is one of the most popular amusement parks in the world. Cedar Point has a beautiful beach, roller coasters, other thrill rides, and a water park, as well as several onsite hotels.

HOCKING HILLS STATE PARK

This 2,356-acre state park is popular with both campers and hikers. Its features include deep gorges, waterfalls, rock shelters, and forested areas.

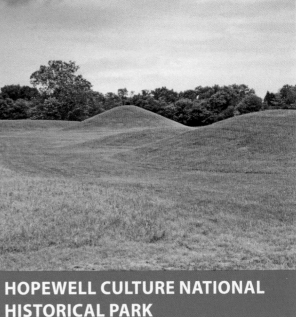

HOPEWELL CULTURE NATIONAL HISTORICAL PARK

Huge burial mounds built by the Hopewell people are a striking feature of this park. One mound is 2,000 years old, and some of the mounds are 12 feet high and 1,000 feet wide.

ROCK AND ROLL HALL OF FAME AND MUSEUM

Located in Cleveland, the Rock and Roll Hall of Fame and Museum has exhibits tracing the history of rock music, memorabilia from many singers and groups, and a gallery dedicated to the artists who have been inducted into the hall.

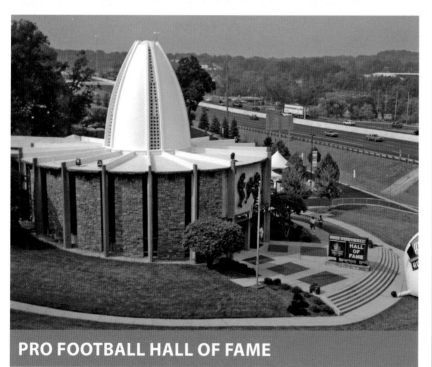

PRO FOOTBALL HALL OF FAME

Visitors to the Pro Football Hall of Fame, in Canton, can learn about the history of football and the National Football League, as well as some of the greats who have played the game.

Industry

From tires to tractors to automobiles, Ohio's industries keep the nation on the move. Before the onset of **industrialization**, the manufacturing of small-scale farm equipment was one of Ohio's main businesses. By the 1890s, Ohioans had developed other important industries besides those linked to agriculture. Today, Ohio is among the nation's manufacturing leaders. The state is a top producer of primary metals, as well as rubber and plastic products.

Industries in Ohio
Value of Goods and Services in Millions of Dollars

Manufacturing makes up a significant part of Ohio's economy. What factors would lead manufacturing to be so important to the state? What types of resources would have to be available in the state for this to occur?

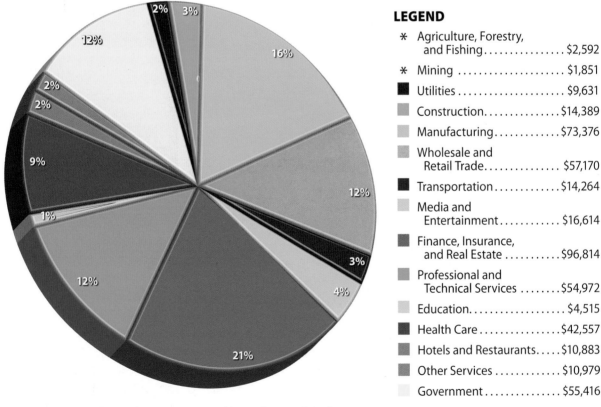

LEGEND

*	Agriculture, Forestry, and Fishing	$2,592
*	Mining	$1,851
	Utilities	$9,631
	Construction	$14,389
	Manufacturing	$73,376
	Wholesale and Retail Trade	$57,170
	Transportation	$14,264
	Media and Entertainment	$16,614
	Finance, Insurance, and Real Estate	$96,814
	Professional and Technical Services	$54,972
	Education	$4,515
	Health Care	$42,557
	Hotels and Restaurants	$10,883
	Other Services	$10,979
	Government	$55,416
	TOTAL	**$466,021**

*Less than 1%. Percentages may not add to 100 because of rounding.

Ohio has a long history in rubber manufacturing and tire production. Charles Goodyear discovered the process of **vulcanizing** rubber in 1839. The tire and rubber company bearing his name was founded in Akron in 1898 and became one of the state's largest firms. Goodyear, which still has its headquarters in Akron, is the top tire manufacturer in North America and Latin America. In 1900, the Firestone Tire & Rubber Company was founded, also in Akron. The Japanese company Bridgestone bought Firestone in 1988, but some facilities remain in Ohio.

The motor vehicle industry employs many Ohioans. Workers assemble vehicles and shape and stamp metal for automobile parts. Metalworkers also manufacture sheet metal, machinery, and tools. In recent years, more Ohioans have been engaged in the aerospace, aviation, and defense industries. **Biotechnology** is also a growing field.

Bridgestone/Firestone, one of the leading tire companies in the world, has a technical center in Akron. Workers there focus on tire research and development.

I DIDN'T KNOW THAT!

Ohio manufactures such transportation equipment as cars, trucks, motorcycles, trailers, and aircraft engines.

In the 1800s, Cincinnati was nicknamed Porkopolis because of its large meat-packing industry.

John Chapman, better known as Johnny Appleseed, brought Ohio settlers apple seeds in the 19th century. The seeds were used to found Ohio's first apple orchards. Apples are now one of the state's highest-yielding fruit crops.

Goodyear Tire & Rubber Company built its first blimp in 1925. Goodyear currently has three blimps in the skies.

Goods and Services

O hio's **civilian** workforce numbers approximately 6 million people. Manufacturing employs about 10 percent of the workforce. Farming now provides jobs for only a small percentage of Ohio's workers, a large shift from the state's early days, when farming was the population's main occupation. The largest segment of the workforce is employed in the service sector, in which workers help or perform a service for people. Nurses, schoolteachers, and bankers are all members of this sector. Transportation and shipping are also important in Ohio's economy. Agricultural and manufactured products are shipped from Ohio to all parts of the United States. Columbus, Cleveland, and Cincinnati are the major trade and transport centers, handling such exports as machinery, transportation equipment, fabricated metals, and rubber products.

The world's only factory dedicated to manufacturing footballs is located in Ada. The Wilson Football factory produces 700,000 footballs each year, including all the balls used by the National Football League.

Corn is Ohio's second most valuable agricultural crop, behind soybeans. More than 3 million acres of corn are planted in the state each year.

Corn and soybeans are Ohio's major crops. Other crops include wheat, hay, tomatoes, apples, grapes, and mushrooms. Ohio is also a major producer of greenhouse and nursery products. Many farms in the state are devoted to floriculture, which is the study of flowers or flowering plants. These farms provide plant bedding, potted flowering plants, and cut flowers.

Ohioans have access to a variety of communication services, as they have many television and radio stations as well as newspapers. The influential Cox and Scripps newspaper chains both began in Ohio in the late 19th century. The state has also been home to some highly acclaimed editors and journalists.

American Indians

People have lived on the land that is now Ohio for at least 11,000 years. Among the early American Indians to settle in the region were those of the Adena culture, which lasted from about 500 BC to 100 AD. The Adena were Ohio's first farmers, and they left behind evidence of settled agricultural settlements, as well as pottery and large ceremonial mounds that can still be seen today. The Hopewell culture thrived in parts of southern and central Ohio. Like the Adena, the Hopewell people were mound builders who created massive structures for worship and social gatherings. They made ornaments from flint, mica, copper, shells, and animal teeth and claws. They lived in the area from about 200 BC to 500 AD. Another group, the Mississippians, lived in the region until about the 1700s.

Pontiac, chief of the Ottawa, led a rebellion against the British in the Ohio Country in 1763. The Indians were defeated. Pontiac made peace with the British a few years later.

By that time, Indians from other areas had begun to settle in what is now Ohio, attracted by its abundant land and **game**. The Mingo, related to the Iroquois, lived in the upper Ohio River Valley. The Shawnee entered from the south, and the Miami from the west. The Ottawa and the Wyandot, also called the Huron, came from the north. Before long, these groups were uprooted and overpowered by the peoples of the well-organized Iroquois **Confederacy**. The confederacy had the first democracy in North America. This meant that all members of the group were given a voice in important decisions. In the years that followed, the Indians experienced conflicts with European explorers and settlers who arrived from the eastern and southern United States.

Indians in the Ohio region used bows and muskets, a type of gun, to hunt fur-bearing animals such as beavers and otters. The Indians received the guns from the Europeans.

Scientists found 700-year-old carvings of human and animal figures on a limestone slab near Lake Erie. The site, on the south shore of Kelleys Island, is now known as Inscription Rock.

In the early 1700s, the Miami people established villages in several river valleys in western Ohio.

In the town of Dublin, an 11-foot-high sculpture of the Wyandot chief Leatherlips was built in 1990.

The Miamisburg Mound, built by the Adena people, is the largest cone-shaped burial mound in Ohio. It was built on a 100 foot high bluff and measures 877 feet in circumference.

The people of the Adena and Hopewell cultures left ornaments, jewelry, tools, and ceramic figurines in their mounds.

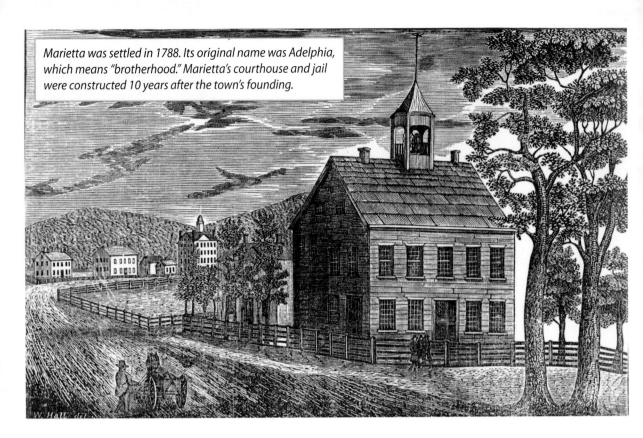

Marietta was settled in 1788. Its original name was Adelphia, which means "brotherhood." Marietta's courthouse and jail were constructed 10 years after the town's founding.

Explorers and Missionaries

The first European known to have arrived in the Ohio River Valley was the French explorer René-Robert Cavelier, sieur de La Salle. He arrived about 1669 and claimed the entire area for France. The French established fur trading with the Indians. Other fur traders, many of them British, began to enter the region in 1685. Missionaries began coming to Ohio in the late 1700s from Germany.

Conflict over control of the fur trade in the area known as the Ohio Country was one of the causes of the French and Indian War. Britain won this war, between France and Britain, in 1763. During the American Revolution, battles were fought in the Ohio area. After the Revolution, the territory became a part of the United States.

Timeline of Settlement

Early Exploration

1669 René-Robert Cavelier, sieur de La Salle, explores the Ohio River Valley and claims the area for France.

1749 Jean-Baptiste Le Moyne, sieur de Bienville, places a series of lead plates along the banks of the Ohio River to show French ownership of the land.

1750 The Ohio Company hires Christopher Gist to survey the land around the Ohio River. Gist provides a detailed description of what is now southern Ohio.

Early Conflicts

1754 The French and Indian War begins. The British, helped by some Indian groups, fight against the French and their Indian allies. An important issue is which nation would control the Ohio Country.

1763 The British win the French and Indian War. They gain control of the Ohio Country.

1763 The British defeat a rebellion led by Ottawa chief Pontiac.

Missions and Early Settlements

1770s Missionaries arrive from Germany and establish several missions in what is now Ohio.

1787 The U.S. Congress passes the Northwest Ordinance, establishing the Northwest Territory, which includes Ohio.

1788 Members of the Ohio Company of Associates found Marietta, the first permanent settlement in the region established by people of European descent.

Territory and Statehood

1790–1794 Settlers and Indians engage in a series of battles, ending with the signing of the Treaty of Greenville in 1795.

1802 President Thomas Jefferson signs the Enabling Act, calling for the admission of Ohio as a state as soon as possible.

1803 Ohio becomes a state.

1812–1813 Ohio is the site of important battles during the War of 1812, including the Battle of Lake Erie.

Early Settlers

Americans from the eastern United States began settling the Ohio area soon after the American Revolution. One of the first acts of the new U.S. government was the Northwest Ordinance. The law opened the area north and west of the Ohio River to orderly settlement. Ohio's earliest communities were built by New Englanders in the Appalachian region and then along the area's major rivers.

Map of Settlements and Resources in Early Ohio

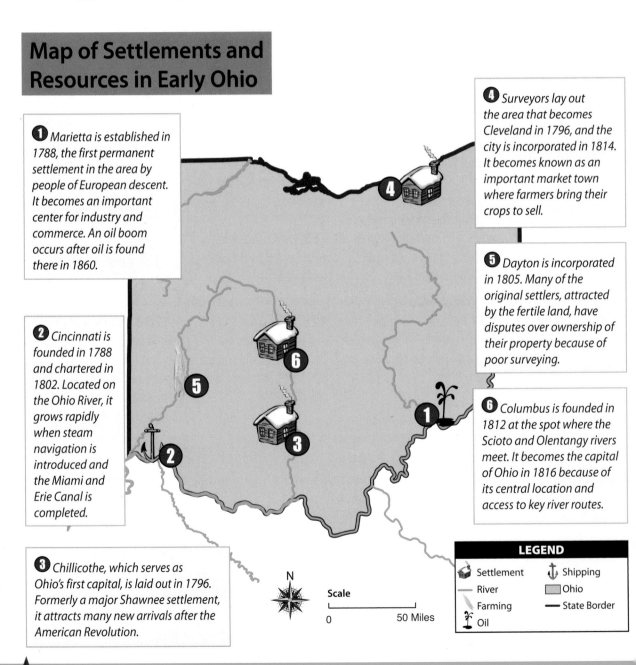

1 Marietta is established in 1788, the first permanent settlement in the area by people of European descent. It becomes an important center for industry and commerce. An oil boom occurs after oil is found there in 1860.

2 Cincinnati is founded in 1788 and chartered in 1802. Located on the Ohio River, it grows rapidly when steam navigation is introduced and the Miami and Erie Canal is completed.

3 Chillicothe, which serves as Ohio's first capital, is laid out in 1796. Formerly a major Shawnee settlement, it attracts many new arrivals after the American Revolution.

4 Surveyors lay out the area that becomes Cleveland in 1796, and the city is incorporated in 1814. It becomes known as an important market town where farmers bring their crops to sell.

5 Dayton is incorporated in 1805. Many of the original settlers, attracted by the fertile land, have disputes over ownership of their property because of poor surveying.

6 Columbus is founded in 1812 at the spot where the Scioto and Olentangy rivers meet. It becomes the capital of Ohio in 1816 because of its central location and access to key river routes.

LEGEND

Settlement		Shipping
River		Ohio
Farming		State Border
Oil		

N

Scale

0   50 Miles

It was not long before the area also became populated by people arriving from different parts of Europe. In the early 1800s, settlers came from Germany, Ireland, France, Scotland, Wales, England, and Sweden. Many Amish and Mennonite settlers came from Switzerland. Ohio's fertile farmlands also began to attract people from other parts of the United States. While New Englanders settled in southeast Ohio, eastern Ohio attracted Quakers from the South and Mid-Atlantic regions. Other people living in the South, including many African Americans, settled in central Ohio. Today, there remains a strong Southern influence in parts of Ohio.

Several **utopian** groups established small, tightly knit communities in Ohio in the early 1800s. One well-known group was the Shakers, a Christian **sect** that attracted followers in the United States in the late 1700s. The Shakers believed in living together without showiness in small farming communities. Another utopian community was that of the Zoarites, a German group that believed in sharing property and responsibility equally among all the members of a community. Their Ohio village, Zoar, lasted from 1817 until 1898.

Cincinnati was founded on the Ohio River in 1788. From a population of 700 in 1790, it grew to nearly 10,000 people by 1820.

I DIDN'T KNOW THAT!

Joseph Smith built the first Mormon temple in the United States in Kirtland, just east of Cleveland, in 1833.

The Shakers made beautiful, simple, and durable furniture. This type of furniture is still manufactured today and is now known as Shaker-style furniture.

The first oil-producing well in the country was drilled near Caldwell in 1814. Unfortunately, the people drilling it were hoping to find salt.

George Armstrong Custer, a U.S. Army cavalry commander, was born in New Rumley in 1839. He was killed in the Battle of the Little Bighorn in 1876.

In the 1850s, most families in Ohio were farm families. The tractor was introduced to Ohio in the early 1900s, making farm work easier than with animal-drawn equipment.

Notable People

Many notable Ohioans contributed to the development of their state and country. Seven U.S. presidents were born in Ohio, more than any other state except Virginia. Prominent Ohioans also include other political leaders and activists for equal rights, some of the nation's leading inventors, and more than 20 U.S. astronauts.

THOMAS EDISON
(1847–1931)

Thomas Edison was born in Milan. He was extremely curious as a child and invented his first device, to transmit telegraph signals, when he was 16. When he was 21, he set up a research laboratory in New Jersey, where he and his employees developed many inventions. They include the incandescent electric light bulb, the phonograph, the carbon microphone, and the kinetoscope, which is a type of motion-picture projector. By the time he died, Edison held the **patents** on 1,093 devices.

WILLIAM HOWARD TAFT
(1857–1930)

William Howard Taft was born in Cincinnati. After graduating from Yale University and Cincinnati Law School, Taft served as a prosecutor and judge. He became Secretary of War in 1904. A Republican, Taft was elected president in 1908. As president, he took steps to limit the power of big business. Taft ran for reelection in 1912 but lost. In 1921, he became chief justice of the U.S. Supreme Court. He is the only person in U.S. history to have served as both president and chief justice.

JOHN GLENN
(1921–)

John Glenn was born in Cambridge. In 1959, he was chosen by NASA, the National Aeronautics and Space Administration, as one of the first seven U.S. astronauts. On February 20, 1962, he became the first American to orbit Earth. Glenn represented Ohio in the U.S. Senate from 1975 to 1999.

CARL STOKES
(1927–1996)

Carl Stokes was born in Cleveland. He was elected to Ohio's House of Representatives in 1962. Five years later, he was elected mayor of Cleveland, becoming the first African American mayor of a major U.S. city. He was elected to a second term. After leaving office, he served as a television newscaster, a judge, and a U.S. ambassador.

NEIL ARMSTRONG
(1930–)

Neil Armstrong was born in Wapakoneta. He became a fighter pilot and a test pilot. He became a NASA astronaut in 1962 and flew his first mission four years later. In 1969, Armstrong commanded the *Apollo 11* moon landing mission. During the mission, on July 20, he became the first person to set foot on the Moon.

I DIDN'T KNOW THAT!

William Tecumseh Sherman (1820–1891) was born in Lancaster. He became a Union general and led troops in some of the most important battles of the Civil War. In 1865, he led his troops in the "march to the sea," through Georgia and the Carolinas.

Gloria Steinem (1934–) was born in Toledo. She became a writer in New York City and was the co-founder of *Ms.* magazine in 1972. She became one of the leading spokespeople for the modern women's movement that began in the late 1960s.

Population

More than 11.5 million people call Ohio home. About 85 percent of the population is of European heritage. African Americans make up about 12 percent of the population, and small numbers of Asian Americans and American Indians also live in the state. Hispanic Americans, who may be of any race, make up about 3 percent of the population. The most ethnically **diverse** region of Ohio is the northeast. This region was the destination of many early **immigrants** from Russia, Eastern Europe, and Italy. Many of these immigrants came to Ohio to work as laborers, often draining swamps and building canals.

Ohio Population 1950–2010

The population of Ohio has grown in every decade since 1950. The sharpest growth was from 1950 to 1960. What factors might have caused the population to increase so rapidly during these years?

Number of People

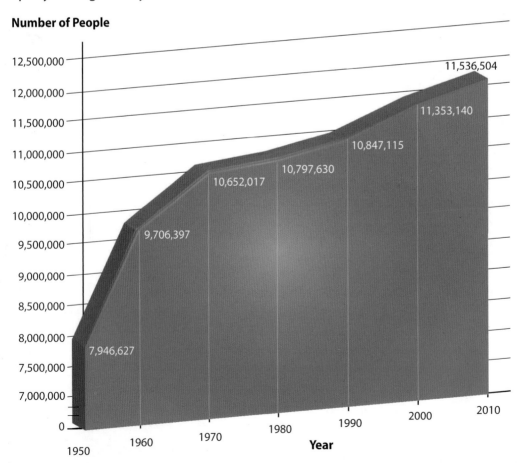

Year	Number of People
1950	7,946,627
1960	9,706,397
1970	10,652,017
1980	10,797,630
1990	10,847,115
2000	11,353,140
2010	11,536,504

Year

Irish, Welsh, and German immigrants also made their way to the state from the East. Some of Ohio's African Americans are the descendants of escaped slaves who made it safely out of the South before the Civil War via the **Underground Railroad**. Columbus is the state's largest city, with a population of more than 760,000. Cleveland is the second-largest, with a population of more than 430,000. There are about 330,000 people in Cincinnati.

The University System of Ohio includes 13 four-year universities and 23 two-year community and technical colleges. One of the main schools in the system is Ohio State University in Columbus, which was founded in 1870. Other state schools are Miami University, Kent State University, and Bowling Green State University. Private schools of higher education include Oberlin College, Antioch College, and Case Western Reserve University.

The Pro Football Hall of Fame in Canton stages a festival every year when new members are inducted. Thousands of people turn out for the parade that goes through downtown Canton.

I DIDN'T KNOW THAT!

The population density of Ohio, which is the number of people per square mile, is more than three times the national average.

Founded in 1833, Oberlin College was the nation's first coeducational college and one of the first to admit African Americans. It was also a station on the Underground Railroad.

Columbus was named the "Best Place to Raise Kids" in the United States by *Business Week* magazine in 2009.

The city of Twinsburg hosts the annual Twins Day Festival every spring, inviting twins to take part in a parade and other events.

From 1820 to 1900, Ohio had the third-largest population in the United States, behind only New York and Pennsylvania.

Politics and Government

Ohio's government, like the federal government of the United States, is divided into three branches. They are the executive, the legislative, and the judicial branches. The executive branch, led by the governor, is responsible for making sure the laws are carried out. Among the governor's many responsibilities is proposing the state budget. The governor and lieutenant governor, along with other public servants such as the secretary of state and attorney general, serve four-year terms. The legislative branch is divided into two parts. The House of Representatives has 99 members who are elected to two-year terms. The Senate has 33 members who are elected to four-year terms. Together, they form the General Assembly, which creates Ohio's laws. The judicial branch interprets laws and governs the court system. Seven judges rule on cases in the state's Supreme Court, which is the highest court in the state. There are also lower-level courts in Ohio.

Construction of the state capitol building, where the state legislature meets, began in 1839. It was completed in 1861. Work often stopped while new funding was arranged.

William McKinley, the 25th president of the United States, who was born in Niles, was one of Ohio's most famous political figures. Elected in 1896 and again in 1900, McKinley expanded U.S. territory overseas during the Spanish-American War. McKinley was a very popular and respected president, but he was **assassinated** in September 1901. Another notable political figure in Ohio politics was John Mercer Langston, who is believed to be the first African American elected to public office in the United States. In 1855, he was elected town clerk of Brownhelm. He later served in the U.S. House of Representatives.

President William McKinley, who was born in Ohio, was assassinated in 1901 by Leon Czolgosz. He was an unemployed factory worker who was an anarchist, a person who thinks all types of government should be abolished.

I DIDN'T KNOW THAT!

Ohio's state song is called "Beautiful Ohio."

Here is an excerpt from the song:

*Beautiful Ohio
I sailed away;
Wandered afar;
Crossed the mighty
restless sea;
Looked for where I ought
to be.
Cities so grand,
mountains above,
Led to this land I love.*

*Beautiful Ohio, where the
golden grain
Dwarf the lovely flowers in the
summer rain.
Cities rising high, silhouette
the sky.
Freedom is supreme in this
majestic land;
Mighty factories seem to hum
in tune, so grand.
Beautiful Ohio, thy wonders
are in view,
Land where my dreams all
come true!*

Cultural Groups

Ohio played an important role in the Underground Railroad and the **abolitionist** movement. Anti-slavery seeds sown in Ohio during the early 1800s helped ignite the Civil War, resulting in the end of slavery. The town of Ripley was an important station on the Underground Railroad. John Rankin, a Presbyterian minister in Ripley, believed deeply in abolition and helped many slaves escape. He formed the Ohio Anti Slavery Society in 1835 and with his family and neighbors, he helped as many as 2,000 people escape bondage. Many African Americans stayed in Ohio, while others went farther north. At Cleveland's African American Museum and at festivals throughout the state, African Americans celebrate their culture. Ohio State University hosts a large African American heritage festival every spring. This festival is a week-long celebration that features African and Caribbean food, music, and poetry.

Caesar's Ford Theatre, in Xenia, produces dramas about Ohio's history that are shown outdoors.

More than 58,000 Amish people live in Ohio, making Ohio the state with the second-largest Amish population. There are 52 individual Amish settlements in the state, most in Holmes County.

The first Mennonite and Amish settlers arrived in the early 1800s. More Mennonites and Amish followed, often transplanting existing communities from Pennsylvania. Many others immigrated directly from Switzerland or elsewhere in Europe. Today, Mennonite groups live in communities across the state, and about one-fourth of all Amish people in the United States live in Ohio. The Amish believe in distancing themselves from the outside world. Members are not allowed to participate in wars or hold public office. They follow a simple, farm-based lifestyle and avoid technology such as electricity, telephones, or automobiles. The followers of the Mennonite faith, on the other hand, tend to be less strict about the use of technology.

I DIDN'T KNOW THAT!

The popular Greek Heritage Festival is held in Cleveland every spring.

Award-winning author Toni Morrison, a well-known Ohioan who was born in Lorain, writes movingly about the lives of African Americans.

The Amish are known for cabinetry, woodworking, and farming with horse-drawn implements.

Cincinnati holds one of the nation's largest Oktoberfest celebrations, bringing together some 500,000 people each year to celebrate the area's German heritage.

Dublin, in central Ohio, attracts Irish people from all over the world to celebrate its annual Dublin Irish Festival. This festival features Irish games, dancing, and musical entertainment.

Arts and Entertainment

Many acclaimed writers have hailed from Ohio. One noted writer who lived in Cincinnati in the 1800s was Harriet Beecher Stowe. She was the author of the novel *Uncle Tom's Cabin*, which raised awareness of the evils of slavery. President Abraham Lincoln is said to have called her "the little woman who started the big war." Other famous Ohio writers include Pulitzer Prize and Nobel Prize winner Toni Morrison, humorist James Thurber, novelist Sherwood Anderson, poet Rita Dove, and children's authors R. L. Stine and Dav Pilkey. Author Zane Grey is best known for his novels and stories set in the Old West.

Film director Steven Spielberg was born in Cincinnati. He has directed some of the most successful films in history, including *Jaws, E.T.,* and *Jurassic Park*. Many actors and actresses hail from Ohio, including television stars Ed O'Neill, Sarah Jessica Parker, and Drew Carey, as well as Oscar winners Halle Berry and Paul Newman. Musicians with Ohio roots include the rap singer Bow Wow and the singers John Legend, Tracy Chapman, and Macy Gray.

Musician and singer John Legend was born in Springfield. He has won numerous Grammy Awards, including best new artist in 2006 and best rhythm and blues album in 2011.

Comedian and actor Drew Carey was born in Cleveland and raised in Parma. In 2007, he began hosting the popular game show The Price Is Right.

Jerry Siegel and Joe Shuster met in Cleveland when they were teenagers. Together, they created the comic book hero Superman in the 1930s.

Talk show host Jerry Springer was a member of the Cincinnati city council and mayor of Cincinnati during the 1970s.

Actress Patricia Heaton, who starred in the TV shows *Everybody Loves Raymond* and *The Middle*, was born in Bay Village and graduated from Ohio State University.

The sharpshooter Annie Oakley, originally named Phoebe Ann Moses, was born in rural Ohio. She had amazing aim and traveled the world in Buffalo Bill's Wild West Show.

The Cleveland Orchestra performs in Cleveland's Severance Hall. The Cincinnati Symphony Orchestra performs in Music Hall.

Sports

O hioans, as well as visitors to the state, have a variety of outdoor activities from which to choose. With the state's wealth of natural areas and state parks, many people enjoy camping, fishing, canoeing, and hiking. A popular destination for outdoor enthusiasts is Wayne National Forest, which covers three separate stretches in the hills of southeastern Ohio. The area sits in the rugged foothills of the Appalachian Mountains and has many lakes, rivers, and streams. Adventurers will likely spot wildlife, including deer, wild turkeys, and a variety of songbirds, in the region. The sport of spelunking, also called caving, can be done in a number of Ohio's caverns. Spelunkers, equipped with flashlights, descend into caves on ropes or on their hands and knees to explore the caves.

The Ohio State Buckeyes have won seven national championships in their 121-year history. In January 2011, they beat the University of Arkansas Razorbacks in the Sugar Bowl by a score of 31–26.

Ohio boasts a number of professional sports teams. The state has two teams in the National Football League, the Cincinnati Bengals and the Cleveland Browns. The Bengals play in Paul Brown Stadium, and the Browns play in Cleveland Browns Stadium on Lake Erie. Ohio's professional baseball teams are the Cincinnati Reds and the Cleveland Indians. The Reds have won the World Series five times, in 1919, 1940, 1975, 1976, and 1990. The Indians have been Cleveland's team since 1915. They have won two World Series championships, in 1920 and in 1948. The Cleveland Cavaliers have been Ohio's National Basketball Association team since 1970, while the Columbus Blue Jackets have been the state's National Hockey League team since 2000. Ohio fans also cheer on the state's college teams. The Ohio State Buckeyes have been especially successful in football and men's basketball.

Joey Votto, who has played first base for the Reds since 2007, won the National League Most Valuable Player award in 2010. He batted .324 with 37 home runs and 113 runs batted in.

I DIDN'T KNOW THAT!

Jesse Owens, who was raised in Cleveland, won four gold medals in track-and-field events at the 1936 Olympic Games.

Golf legend Jack Nicklaus is from Columbus. He won 18 major championships during his career.

The National Football League got its start in Canton in 1920.

The Reds' home field is the Great American Ballpark in Cincinnati. The team has played under various names throughout its history, including the Red Stockings and the Redlegs.

The Cincinnati Red Stockings were baseball's first professional team. They had a perfect season in 1869, winning all 57 games they played.

Pitcher Cy Young, who won more games than anyone else in baseball history, was born in Gilmore. The Cy Young Award is given to the best pitchers in baseball each year.

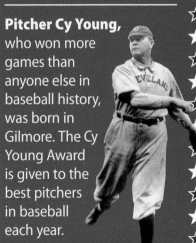

National Averages Comparison

T he United States is a federal republic, consisting of fifty states and the District of Columbia. Alaska and Hawai'i are the only non-contiguous, or non-touching, states in the nation. Today, the United States of America is the third-largest country in the world in population. The United States Census Bureau takes a census, or count of all the people, every ten years. It also regularly collects other kinds of data about the population and the economy. How does Ohio compare to the national average?

Comparison Chart

United States 2010 Census Data *	USA	Ohio
Admission to Union	NA	March 1, 1803
Land Area (in square miles)	3,537,438.44	40,948.38
Population Total	308,745,538	11,536,504
Population Density (people per square mile)	87.28	281.73
Population Percentage Change (April 1, 2000, to April 1, 2010)	9.7%	1.6%
White Persons (percent)	72.4%	82.7%
Black Persons (percent)	12.6%	12.2%
American Indian and Alaska Native Persons (percent)	0.9%	0.2%
Asian Persons (percent)	4.8%	1.7%
Native Hawaiian and Other Pacific Islander Persons (percent)	0.2%	—
Some Other Race (percent)	6.2%	1.1%
Persons Reporting Two or More Races (percent)	2.9%	2.1%
Persons of Hispanic or Latino Origin (percent)	16.3%	3.1%
Not of Hispanic or Latino Origin (percent)	83.7%	96.9%
Median Household Income	$52,029	$48,011
Percentage of People Age 25 or Over Who Have Graduated from High School	80.4%	83.0%

*All figures are based on the 2010 United States Census, with the exception of the last two items.

How to Improve My Community

Strong communities make strong states. Think about what features are important in your community. What do you value? Education? Health? Forests? Safety? Beautiful spaces? Government works to help citizens create ideal living conditions that are fair to all by providing services in communities. Consider what changes you could make in your community. How would they improve your state as a whole? Using this concept web as a guide, write a report that outlines the features you think are most important in your community and what improvements could be made. A strong state needs strong communities.

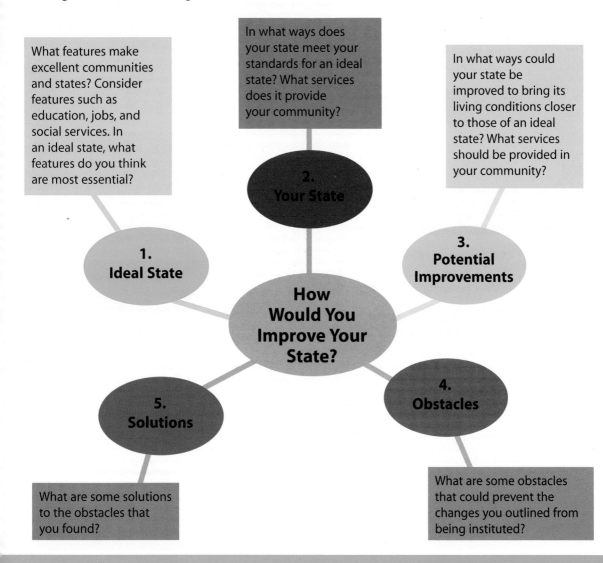

What features make excellent communities and states? Consider features such as education, jobs, and social services. In an ideal state, what features do you think are most essential?

In what ways does your state meet your standards for an ideal state? What services does it provide your community?

In what ways could your state be improved to bring its living conditions closer to those of an ideal state? What services should be provided in your community?

2. Your State

1. Ideal State

3. Potential Improvements

How Would You Improve Your State?

5. Solutions

4. Obstacles

What are some solutions to the obstacles that you found?

What are some obstacles that could prevent the changes you outlined from being instituted?

Exercise Your Mind!

Think about these questions and then use your research skills to find the answers and learn more fascinating facts about Ohio. A teacher, librarian, or parent may be able to help you locate the best sources to use in your research.

1 *What was Ohio resident Thomas Edison famous for inventing?*

a. the gasoline-powered car
b. the incandescent lightbulb
c. the television
d. the computer

2 A well-known entertainer comes from Cincinnati. Who is he?

3 Did Orville and Wilbur Wright fly the first aircraft in their home state of Ohio?

4 Ohioans John Glenn and Neil Armstrong were what kind of explorers?

a. polar explorers
b. mountain climbers
c. space explorers
d. deep-sea explorers

5 One of the Great Lakes touches Ohio. Which one is it?

6 Which Washington, D.C., monument was designed by a young Ohio architect?

7 Who "jumped" into the spotlight at the 1924 Olympic Games in Paris?

8 Cleveland is said to be the home of:

a. rock climbing
b. rock and roll
c. Rock Hudson
d. rock lobster

Words to Know

abolitionist: a person who worked to end slavery in the United States

assassinated: murdered, often for political reasons

aviation: the design, development, production, and operation of aircraft

biotechnology: the use of microorganisms or biological substances to perform industrial or manufacturing processes

civilian: not military

confederacy: an alliance between groups for mutual assistance and protection

conifers: trees, such as evergreens and shrubs, that bear their seeds and pollen on separate, cone-shaped structures

diverse: different or varied

endangered: in danger of dying out

game: wild animals hunted for food or sport

glaciers: large masses of slow-moving ice

immigrants: people who move to a new country

industrialization: the process of switching from an agricultural way of life to mechanized industry

patents: legal documents giving the person who invented something the sole right to make or sell it

reservoirs: lakes, often artificial, for collecting water

sect: a group of people with the same beliefs who follow the same leader

sedimentary: a type of rock formed by layers that have been pressed together

species: a group of animals or plants that share the same characteristics and can mate

Underground Railroad: a secret network in the United States in the 19th century that helped slaves escape to freedom

utopian: believing in the possibility of building an ideal place with a perfect social system

vulcanizing: making rubber hard and durable enough to use for vehicle tires

Index

African Americans 34, 38

agriculture 11, 22, 23, 24, 25, 31

Akron 7, 23

American Indians 20, 26, 27, 28, 29

Amish 5, 31, 39

Armstrong, Neil 33

Cincinnati 7, 30, 39

Cleveland 4, 7, 20, 30, 38, 39

coal 14, 15

Columbus 5, 7, 9, 30, 34

Dayton 7, 21, 30

Edison, Thomas 32

fur trade 27, 28

Glenn, John 33

Lake Erie 6, 7, 8, 10, 15

limestone 14, 15

McKinley, William 37

Mennonites 31, 39

minerals 14, 15

Morrison, Toni 39, 40

Ohio River 6, 7, 8, 15

Rock and Roll Hall of Fame and Museum 4, 20, 21

rubber 22, 23

Stokes, Carl 33

Taft, William Howard 32

Toledo 7, 21

Wright brothers 5

Log on to www.av2books.com

AV² by Weigl brings you media enhanced books that support active learning. Go to www.av2books.com, and enter the special code found on page 2 of this book. You will gain access to enriched and enhanced content that supplements and complements this book. Content includes video, audio, web links, quizzes, a slide show, and activities.

Audio
Listen to sections of the book read aloud.

Video
Watch informative video clips.

Embedded Weblinks
Gain additional information for research.

Try This!
Complete activities and hands-on experiments.

WHAT'S ONLINE?

Try This!

Test your knowledge of the state in a mapping activity.

Find out more about precipitation in your city.

Plan what attractions you would like to visit in the state.

Learn more about the early natural resources of the state.

Write a biography about a notable resident of Ohio.

Complete an educational census activity.

Embedded Weblinks

Discover more attractions in Ohio.

Learn more about the history of the state.

Learn the full lyrics of the state song.

Video

Watch a video introduction to Ohio.

Watch a video about the features of the state.

EXTRA FEATURES

Audio
Listen to sections of the book read aloud.

Key Words
Study vocabulary, and complete a matching word activity.

Slide Show
View images and captions and prepare a presentation.

Quizzes
Test your knowledge.

AV² was built to bridge the gap between print and digital. We encourage you to tell us what you like and what you want to see in the future.

Sign up to be an AV² Ambassador at www.av2books.com/ambassador.

Due to the dynamic nature of the Internet, some of the URLs and activities provided as part of AV² by Weigl may have changed or ceased to exist. AV² by Weigl accepts no responsibility for any such changes. All media enhanced books are regularly monitored to update addresses and sites in a timely manner. Contact AV² by Weigl at 1-866-649-3445 or av2books@weigl.com with any questions, comments, or feedback.